A daughter remembers Dylan

CHRISTMAS AND OTHER MEMORIES

by
Aeronwy Thomas

ISBN 1 872560 17 2

This publication is a revised and expanded edition of a booklet first published by Amwy Press Ltd in 1978 to mark the twentyfifth anniversary of the death of Dylan Thomas.

MERTON BOOKS
PO Bo 279, Twickenham TW1 4XQ
Tel: 0208 892 4949
www.mertonbooks.co.uk

CONTENTS

ACKNOWLEDGEMENTS

The extract from "Prologue", by Dylan Thomas, is included by permission of David Higham Associates and is published in *Collected Poems* (Dent).
"Later than Laugharne", was previously published in *Rooks and Poems,* by Aeronwy Thomas, published by Poetry Monthly Press.
Two of the articles, 'Christmas - when Dad showed goodwill toward children' and 'Our poisonous tea party' were first published in *The Western Mail.*

Prologue

This day winding down now
At God speeded summer's end
In the torrent salmon sun,
In my seashaken house
On a breakneck of rocks
Tangled with chirrup and fruit,
Froth, flute, fin and quill
At a wood's dancing hoof,
By scummed, starfish sands
With their fishwife cross
Gulls, pipers, cockles, and sails,
Out there, crow black, men
Tackled with clouds, who kneel
To the sunset nets,
Geese nearly in heaven, boys
Stabbing, and herons, and shells
That speak seven seas,
Eternal waters away
From the cities of nine
Days' night whose towers will catch
In the religious wind
Like stalks of tall, dry straw,
At poor peace I sing
To you, strangers, (though song
Is a burning and crested act,
The fire of birds in
The world's turning wood,
For my sawn, splay sounds),
Out of these seathumbed leaves
That will fly and fall
Like leaves of trees and as soon
Crumble and undie
Into the dogdayed night.

Dylan Thomas

Christmas
When Dad showed goodwill toward children

My memories of Christmas spent with my family at Laugharne, at the now famous family home, "The Boat House", began with a bang.

Luckily my mother was never a spoil sport, and she filled our stockings with things that squeaked, whistled and trumpeted: rubbery toys, whistles and trumpets that whined metallically and magically.

My two brothers, Llewelyn (three years older) and Colm (the baby) could never match my attention-catching and squeaking, banging and trumpet wailings. I snatched their stocking presents from resisting fingers to add to my own assembled cacophony of "musical" instruments amidst their howls of protest.

The noise must have been terrible enough to send my peace-loving father sloping off to his work shed at the other end of the cliff walk. But not at Christmas.

Christmas Day, as I remember it, was a day where normal habits and routine were temporarily waived and we, the children, came into our own. We were allowed to bully my father for an hour or so before he gingerly made his way off to Brown's pub, 20 minutes walk from the house.

Before joining the festive crowd in the pub, he would cross the road to The Pelican, the house his parents inhabited in their last years. I cannot remember if my grandparents shared Christmas with us at The Boat House.

As they were such an integral part of my childhood, they might have faded in my memory. I can remember Christmas more for the general excitement due to my father's unaccustomed presence and participation.

One Christmas he returned with an enormous doll's house which preceded him, by an arm's length, as he delicately stepped his way down the precipitous flagstone steps of the garden path. He broke his arm so often that we all waited with baited breath to see whether he would fall again to have his arm placed in its habitual gypsy scarf, Nelson style across his chest.

My mother maintains the Thomas family had "chicken bones". Granny Thomas, as we knew her, constantly fractured arms and legs. However, my father's extreme care of the doll's house circumvented another accident.

He and the huge doll's house arrived as far as the front door where he deposited it. We fingered and commented on many apertures, bits of furniture all jumbled together and the sectioned off rooms.

Anyone could see it was for me, the only girl in the family, and I cannot remember being more touched by any other one event (and that was 50 years ago!).

This gesture of my father's was most unusual for its physical effort, something to be avoided at all costs with a strong Irish wife who loved movement of all types. When it came to lugging the coal left in sacks outside his shed the services of an odd job man were enlisted.

Christmas in our house started with stockings and the bigger presents were given out after lunch, so the aim was to get to that moment as speedily as possible.

The weather was always bleak, cold and damp and I can never remember any exciting, lovely snow as we trudged to church (unaccompanied by adults) for the morning service.

My mother waited for us, on our return, for a long walk before lunch. It was called by her our "penance" and felt like one as we tried to keep up with her as she took great strides and lungfulls of damp sea and country air.

But after a while the walk acquired the magic it always did and we followed our usual trail across Sir John's Hill. Our return "loop", another of my mother's expressions, took us along the shingle and mudflats of the estuary, with overhead the castle walls and the cliffwalk with the occasional person or dog peering over at us and the estuary. The last part of the long walk took us along the rocks which we shinned to avoid sinking in the mud which surrounded the Boat House.

It was always lovely to get home out of the low-lying, swirling mists of the cold winter day. By this time, my father had returned from his indoor pub revelries ready for lunch cooked by our "treasure" Dolly.

At Christmas we all ate together. My father's aversion to the noise of children, whereby he ate separately, was forgotten today. This aversion was normally so strong that when we travelled in trains my mother and children were banished to one carriage while my father travelled in another - a bag of sweets in one hand, a good thriller in another.

On Christmas Day, the entire family ate in the dining room with a huge coal fire roaring in the grate, the holly over the mantelpiece singed at the edges. I loved the dining room, a small cosy room with the table and the chairs painted a shiny blue.

The same pot of paint must have provided new skins for the two sheds and the garden gate and the outside woodwork of the house. A sideboard, also blue, had ornate plates and china dogs when they were still not considered collectors' items. On occasion my mother would raid the housekeeping money to buy Staffordshire dogs and plates depicting places from a travelling salesman who set up shop in a nearby house. She could not resist pretty china.

After a traditional lunch: turkey, sprouts, mashed swede and potato, we opened our presents. These were nearly always books chosen by my father. Some of the books I can recall were *The Wind in the Willows,* Arthur Ransome books for Llewelyn, Baba, Dickens (of course) and especially for me Mary Poppins and Enid Blyton, because none of us knew she was uneducational.

From America, my father brought us many books, such as the marvellous illustrated books posing questions like, "Who gave us catherine wheels?" and you turn the page to see slant-eyed Oriental children holding the spluttering wheels in their hands.

I loved these books. My father would often read to me, but always books of his own choice. We both favoured *Grimms' Fairy Tales.* He would enact the main characters becoming the wolf or the simpering little child, giving creditable characterisations of good and evil. We both relished the thrill of horror and fear that Grimm's never fails to invoke.

"Read to me, read to me," I would scream at every opportunity. My father reading to me was my special ground with him and has given me the conviction of sharing a special relationship. This is a conviction held by others about themselves, I believe.

Throughout all the excitement of opening presents, my father and I ate sweets. It was a communal passion. Boiled sweets included the old-fashioned humbugs with beige, white and liver-coloured stripes, and were my father's delight.

Mine were liquorice and sherbet. I can never remember being told to eat fewer sweets in our house, and so grew rounder and more like my father every day.

After lunch, and presents and sweets and more sweets, we started on games. My father had had music in his day with his father quite an accomplished pianist but none of us were musical.

You could say words in any and every form had taken over from the music. My father and his father would do the crossword every morning before crossing the road for the first pints of beer.

My father involved everyone in his overriding interest in words. To have married a man whose main interest is choral music offers not only a change from my background but a constant source of refreshment for me.

The games my father enjoyed most were unsurprisingly based on words, so charades were played. His choice of words in spite of being brilliantly acted were rather difficult for us.

My own choice was always the same: macaroni and spaghetti and it amazed me how everyone guessed them straight away year after year. When we all got overtired, and started to quarrel among ourselves, my mother would stop us. One time, a crate sent all the way from California by a fan or friend of my father's was opened at this stage to reveal exotic dried fruit inside. We all pounced on it...... but I was beginning to feel rather full. When our exuberance, refuelled by the short rest, could be contained no longer we started playing our favourite Blind Man's Buff in which our hysterical dog, Mably, took an important role, biting everyone's ankles. This was the time my father usually chose to make a move.

With my father out of the house, at Brown's waiting for my mother, games were followed by a noisy bedtime session. I tried not to delay my mother. My new books and my torch lay in waiting.

My mother would soon be leaving and there were no babysitters in those days, luckily. On reading my father's reminiscences years later I was surprised to see how he had read books by torchlight too. The characters seem to take life of their own at night, and I listened with relief to the front door closing as my mother departed in one of her quilted, swirling skirts.

Maybe they would return, as they did some years, with friends, stumbling down the unlit path and maybe mother would dance, Isadora Duncan style.

Now where's my torch? I thought, fumbling in the dark, and once again before I could enter my make-believe world of words and mull over the wonderful Christmas Day, I would fall asleep.

Reading with Dad

If I could catch my dad after his bath, he would read to me. Comfortably ensconced in a capacious armchair, on his lap, he would read me stories and rhymes of his choice. From my vantage point I could see the estuary through the slats of the balcony but shut out all distractions to listen to Dad. Was it going to be Grimms' *Fairy Tales* or *the Old Woman Who Lived in a Shoe* with all the children. Heaven, it was going to be *Little Red Riding Hood.* "Who would you like to be?" he asked. "You're so good as the wolf," I replied, "so you can play him and the woodchopper." Of course, I was left with the title role, if Dad agreed. Soon we were in the wood with the nasty wolf hiding behind trees and the poor girl in her red cape visible to all. Dad made me read all the dialogue which I pretended was a little difficult for my reading skills. "I only know the easy words," I lied. I made myself easy in the armchair, sitting on his lap as if I owned him.

Another session we read Hansel and Gretel and I was forced to run around looking for matches. "This is the place the children slept when they first ran away from their nasty family," he said, pouring a mound of matches on the floor. I didn't think they looked much like a leafy mound to serve as a bed but did not like to say so. He then made an outline with matches of the witches' cottage made from sweets to tempt Hansel and Gretel. What about the cauldron or oven to cook them, I demanded. He placed his beer glass in the house, which didn't convince me. "What about something smaller?" I asked. Finally, to my satisfaction, he poured out the dolly mixture he kept in his pocket into the sweet house and I fashioned an oven from a piece of plasticine. There followed a debate about who should play the witch and the less interesting characters of the children. In the end, Dad adopted a falsetto voice adding words that I knew were not on the page and made quite a convincing evil old lady. I might ask him to wear a hat from our dress-up box another time, I thought.

Dad could also make lots of other characters from fairytale and nursery rhyme come alive. There was the gruff Giant in *Jack and the Beanstalk* and the jumpy white rabbit from *Alice in*

Wonderland, read in a staccato, neurotic voice. Aladdin had a similar voice to the witch one without the frightening tones. It was the best time of the week when Dad opened a book with me.

Always one to sieze the moment, I would lurk outside the bathroom door where you could hear him try out different characters from *Under Milk Wood* such as Mrs Dai Bread One and Mrs Dai Bread Two. As the bath was newly installed thanks to a patron, both my parents spent a long time there topping up the hot water. We, the children, had to make do with the tin bath in front of the Aga. As he emerged, hot and steamy, I would pounce with my reading requests, nipping into the bathroom to see whether his detective novel had fallen into the bath water or mainly to fish out any sweets he might have left. I can remember once Mother, who was impatient to get out for their every night pub session, walking in while we were reading from *Struwwelpeter*, waving a pair of scissors to cut Dad's toenails. We were delighted with the timing and asked Mother to try and not cut off his toes as well.

Interior of the writing shed - the "water and tree room".

Photo: Courtesy of Alan Shepherd

Train journey with my father

I can remember how my father used to compartmentalise his life never allowing one area to overlap into another. This was especially true when we rarely travelled by train as a family. My father would disappear to leave the rest of the family to cope without him. Mother on her own had to orchestrate the screams and wails of her demanding children. Llewelyn and I fought (sometimes), wanted drinks and sandwiches as well as endless entertainment: the usual guessing games and quiet reading, the latter suggested by mother when we became too loud and enthusiastic for fellow passengers. Colm, a youngster, would also join in the fun.

My father meantime sat in blessed peace in another carriage, reading his thrillers and dining on half a pound of boiled sweets. On one journey in the late forties, I was sent to tell him we were almost at our destination and to return to the family unit. I found him in the buffet drinking beer and eating a sandwich. Mother had given us children home-made sandwiches and I briefly resented his shop-bought ones which looked much neater and more desirable than mother's doorstep versions of mashed hard-boiled egg with beetroot which had a tendency to fall out and stain our clothes. In those days anything bought in the shop (clothes, cakes or fizzy drinks) was prized over the second best home imitations.

My father made me wait while he finished his conversation with the barman, another bar mate chipping in with his contribution. When the train drew up at Paddington, emitting a lovely sound of steam and an expiry of breath reminiscent of a huge mammal dying, we had to dismount onto the platform straightaway, my father helping me only when I reminded him of my presence and could not quite manage the high steps. Mother arrived dragging bags and Colm, my father only noticing her at the last moment possible, excusing himself with the onerous task he had of helping me off the train. My mother said a few choice words to him but delivered without much passion, merely as a formality to express her disapproval. She knew my father well. It was she who suggested in the train that he decamp and find himself somewhere away from the children and their noise. It was my mother who directed us to be quiet as we passed the cliff walk shed in Laugharne where he worked on his poems and to keep out of the dining room while she and my father ate their meals. As children we also understood and did not resent being separated from our parents in this way.

In fact, we quite enjoyed the freedom it gave us. As my mother and father ate in The Boat House in the room next door, the children supervised by our treasure Dolly, we could eat, chat and laugh unchecked in the kitchen. We ate the sort of food we liked at the scrubbed deal table with no-one counting how many other friends we could add to our number. Dolly always made extra chips and fried eggs when required while mother and father ate proper, boring food. This was often one of mother's Irish stews, the same one boiled up before every meal until mother considered it looked suspect when it changed to a slightly green colour and was thrown away. Every day new vegetables were added to the stew with the same butcher's bone simmering in the depths. Dolly always cooked different food for the Thomas children. There were advantages we felt to my father's need to eat separately from us and learned not to resent the way he sectioned his life into manageable areas so that he remained undisturbed by family when working, eating or socialising.

Dylan in 1937, 23 years old and just married.

Photo: Courtesy of Jeff Towns/Dylan's Bookstore

Our poisonous tea party for an amorous student

The path going down to the Boat House winds its way precipitously down the cliff side, bordering what was once our front garden. It ends at the front door of the modest, sea swept house which was once our home, 25 years ago.

Now the Boat House has been made into a museum to honour my father's genius and tourists make the long trek to visit the house and the sea town of Laugharne, West Wales. We lived as a family miles from any large town, surrounded by some of the most beautiful sea and country landscape in Wales, unaware that our time was limited and to be curtailed by my father's death in 1953.

I remember it was quite a long walk to and from the village, or town as it calls itself. The distance used to discourage some school friends from joining me after school, and in retrospect they might have been stopped by their parents as the Boat House was one of the unsafest places imaginable for children. Alterations made since my time have minimised major hazards. My two brothers Llewelyn (three years older) and Colm (six years younger) and I, together with friends willing to brave the perils, were blissfully unaware of all dangers. Maybe we learned to deal with them instead.

Revisiting Laugharne as an adult it turns out to be a mere five minute walk along the cliff walk before you reach my father's old shed where he used to write. Painted a lively blue, it is perched there with its view of the estuary and a minute's walk takes me to another shed, similar in appearance, where we used to keep our bikes. I look over the railings where the cliffside constantly threatens to crumble and see below the roof and front of our one-time home. Then turning the end corner of a stone wall, sprouting with grasses and wild flowers I open a wooden gate, also painted bright blue.

As I look down the serpentine path at the grassy ledges which form a sort of garden called grandly by us the front garden and see once again the low stone wall which is there to keep one from falling over the edge onto the estuary floor, I am transported back to my childhood.

We who lived there soon learned the art of the mountain goat, and cloven hooved would run down the path, jumping over the steps which jut out of the earth at intervals, and become skating arenas in bad weather, resting a moment to regain footing and on again leaping and bounding down the path to home.

We learned to clamber all over the house up and down the narrow staircases, and the various wooden balconies (constantly renewable because of the corroding salt air). We ran along the top surface of the surrounding walls with their uneven stones and like monkeys clambered all over the rocks which lay along the seashore.

No doubt my father would have had more visitors if he had chosen to live somewhere more accessible, but for me there were still too many of them to take him away from his family. Intense, foreign students studying my father's life and works for their degrees, or American "friends" and acquaintances who showered us with gifts, were frequent visitors. They would look at us with unconcealed amazement as we children skipped along the top of a wall or vaulted over the outside loo roof on to the wooden balcony which embraced our house, often treating us like little savages.

Our resentment of their intrusion into our lives took different forms. I can remember inviting a very good looking Scandinavian to partake of tea with me. "Everyone comes to tea with me," I assured him, and as he was still unsure, added, "My father would expect it of you." Taking tea consisted of sitting behind a shed out of view in the company of all my teddies and one of my girlfriends. The beverage was a purple coloured juice and the edibles some berries.

Politely he partook of the berry tea, looking rather uncomfortable on a piece of rock with jagged edges specially reserved for him. Solemnly, with the conscientious and serious demeanour of all the students we had seen at our house he ate every berry, every one we hoped more poisonous. He did not go into convulsions or die as we half hoped but was ill enough to have to leave. A small price to pay, I thought, for flirting with my mother.

As far as I remember I was never punished. Discipline in our house must have seemed erratic to our visitors. My mother rarely nagged us about possible physical dangers lurking everywhere and allowed us to bring as many of our friends to play as we liked. Any punishment was meted out on the spot with a series of hits on the head. "I can remember your father only ever hitting one of you children," my mother told me, "And that was you."

Apparently, I would infuriate my parents to gain their attention. In fact, my father refused to reprimand us, verbally or physically, as he considered this my mother's role. I can never remember him raising his voice, let alone hitting anyone.

This attitude extended to his refusal to eat with his children. He hated the noise and presumably wished to avoid having to shout at us. We were delighted. The children were made to eat in the kitchen making as much bedlam as they chose, and chose plenty, while my parents ate in the dining room with the door closed. We were allowed cider on the principle that cider is not alcoholic while the grownups had beer. Of course, the noise in the kitchen where we ate with as many cronies as we could jam in, became worse as more cider was consumed.

A perfect example illustrating my parents varying attitudes: I lay in bed with a severe case of mumps, ants walking in colonies over the wall in my delirium, when my parents started to row over something. My mother raged and ranted while my father expostulated quietly. This ended with my mother throwing a slipper at my father who was standing by my bed. His only form of resistance was to duck, allowing the slipper to hit me. It would have been quite out of keeping with his passive temperament to throw the slipper back.

This sort of rowing never upset me. We were used to it, and it did not threaten the stability of our home. What was more insidious were the steadily more frequent absences of my father from home as he pursued the promised crock of gold in America. My mother would react in a sullen, untypical way on my father's return. Her silences after an initial verbal outburst were infinitely worse than any throwing of slippers. Even as a child I began to feel some change in the air. At the age of 10, my mother sent me to boarding school in England to train as a dancer, a chance *she* always wanted, but which I saw as a rejection of sorts by my family. Already Llewelyn was a boarder at Magdalen College School at Oxford and only came home for holidays and my father was away in America on his third reading tour during that fateful year of 1953. Only my mother and Colm remained in Laugharne.

It was while I was at school, settling in and beginning to enjoy the delights of the ballet and allied arts that my aunt, Nicolette Devas, brought me the news of my father's death. It was some time before I realised that our days in Laugharne were virtually over: my mother could not bear to return there without my father, and we only went back a couple more times. I could feel my mother's bewilderment and distress over my father's death, and will never blame her for wanting to live the following years, now a quarter of a century, away from Wales in Rome and Sicily, as far as she could go from the memories of our family life there.

◇◇◇

Photo: Douglas Glass

Ferryboat in Laugharne. Aeronwy being handed to her mother, Dylan watching.

Dylan and Caitlin in London
Chelsea pub haunts 1943 to 2005

A small group of us, some from Wales, others the suburbs of London, met to do the Chelsea Pub Tour. This was a route devised by John Ackerman, Dylan Thomas' biographer, to recapture the haunts regularly frequented by the poet and his wife, Caitlin. Beer was in short supply during the War so often in an evening they would visit two or more of the pubs on our itinerary in the hopes of fresh supplies.

From Sloane Square where we convened we walked along King's Rd. towards the Town Hall. On the way we passed the Markham Arms by Markham Square where my Aunt Nicolette, Caitlin's sister, used to live with her husband, portrait painter Anthony Devas. "It's become the HSBC bank," I exclaimed. Returning to Markham Sq. I recalled that when the Thomases arrived to stay in the basement for a longer period than welcome the Markham Arms was their local. We move on.

Just past the Town Hall, on that side of the road, lies another popular pub, the Six Bells, which I can remember on my visits to my aunt, then at Carlyle Square, as a rather dark establishment smelling of stale beer and sawdust underfoot. Inside it's now a disinfectant, plastic place with an American theme selling burgers and upmarket bottled lagers. The garden, however, is much more to our taste in our search of what was and we sit at the wooden slatted tables with welcome outdoor heaters needed most of the year, a fountain of old stone that must be an original, tinkling centre stage. I point out to my friends as we carry our first drinks to the tables, pulling scarves and mitts on closer, that the fence one side was John Ackerman's shared garden flat where he would occasionally entertain in the Summer. I apologise to him wherever he is, continuing my trip down the past. "Can't imagine my parents here with all these changes," I complain. "They boasted that they always sat through the air raid warnings, the sirens screeching, disturbing, but never interrupting the talk. "We were the brave ones," my mother said, "never taking refuge in the basements along King's Road."

Fortified by a rather too large gin for such an early hour, I suggest after a while walking to Cheyne Walk along the Embankment to find the Eight Bells pub there. As we pass a blue plaque on a tall house, I remembered John's stock-in-trade John Carlyle anecdote to the effect that Carlyle was so boring when he started to expound a topic with no conclusion that reputedly his dog threw himself out of an upper window in despair. My friends all looked up at the house no doubt wondering from which window the impatient dog had flung itself. We move on.

Arriving at the Eight Bells – or rather where it used to stand – I look around as if it might be hiding somewhere. But no – it's an exclusive bistro it says – and I bang crossly at the closed door. A waiter in top hat and tails opens the heavy portal making me feel short and unsmart in my black trousers and mock suede jacket... not to mention the flat suede booties. I ask what's happened to the Eight Bells. Suddenly, he becomes more affable but still hasty: "It's a private reception. See, a wedding buffet." We all get a glimpse of linen clad tables and bridal green and white flora looped round the edges.

Disappointed not to meet the shadow of Mum and Dad, not to feel something of their presence lingering over the ensuing years since they left, I suggest The Cross Keys, our next destination just round the corner. We all brace ourselves for another change for the worse, the cleaned-up refurbished pub. To think John's tours only a few years ago included proper pub stops at all of them but there it is the welcoming pub front a wall of statuary that dates back to their time. White swans in alabaster nudge fantastical creatures there to tempt the pub goer – a large pair of crossed keys the centrepiece to deck the wall relief. We enter, order a drink at the bar and sit at a table to wait. Blessedly, no music plays.

My parents join us and my friends from Wales are quick to offer them a drink. Not long and other friends of theirs greet us all. We move along to make more room...my father still at the bar. It is becoming a jolly party. "Will you be eating," queries the man behind the bar. Mother looks up shocked. She's not used to eating while you drink. "Well, that's an improvement on my day," she says. "I was always starving in the days we went drinking. Dylan never seemed to worry. Theodora (Fitzgibbon) used to prepare a stew in a bucket when she lived in Paris. She wrote cookery books after that." "That was a very good idea...so at least at the end of a hard night's drinking, you could heat up a lamb stew with root veg and potatoes." She stopped her flow to take a draught of her beer, a Guinness (hard to get during the War). She looked at me. "How are you doing? Who are these friends of your's?" her voice fading before I could answer and all the raucous crowd dwindling to just us four as we ordered pub snacks all round.

"Well, at least we found them," said my friend Reg from Bridgend. "I was beginning to think too much water under the bridge... since that time. Soon we'll be joining them somewhere else," he commented philosophically. "I wonder if there are pubs there..." and to make himself clearer, said, "Up there," pointing heavenward. I laughed, unsure whether heaven would be a place of no hangovers (only pub sessions that reminded them of Cross Keys). "Oh, let's move on," said my husband Trefor, impatiently. "Where to?"

"To The Anglesey, off Fulham Rd. It's a bit of a walk." When we last went there on John's tour we took along a Spanish student staying at our house – John and Juan got on famously. He told John – not us though we'd been together for a week – that he hungered for the bright lights of the town, Barcelona, in his case, and intended to study there. I told this story to an unresponsive audience. What they really wanted on a Dylan and Caitlin tour was to see them again. "Well," I said not wishing to raise hopes, "We'll have to see whether The Anglesey's still there, first."

"It's known as The Welsh Club," Trefor explained as we all sat down at one of the deal tables outside. He was about to tell them that rugby teams from Wales made The Anglesey their regular pub when on a visit from the Principality or God's Country, his usual joke. A roar of laughter from inside the pub stopped his train of thought (stopped him in mid sentence). We looked round the door... what we saw was going to make Reg and Eileen very happy... a fitting end for the tour.

Dad was standing there, at the bar, a pint by his right hand, surrounded by a crowd. Aunt Nicolette, I could see, was trying to get his attention. Reg offered her a drink which she took gratefully, and all were quiet as they listened to the raconteur. Story after story followed - it was getting late – everyone laughing, drinking, keeping the barman happy. "Time," he shouted, "Beer's run out." and everyone drifted away chuckling to themselves, helping each other down the step so that only Nicolette and us were left. Caitlin was nowhere to be seen. Mother had told me this story so many times I could predict Nicolette's next words: "Oh no, I quite forgot my message... Caitlin's waiting in the hospital for you to visit her and your new baby daughter. She's been in a week and is due out tomorrow." Dad looked startled, guilty and frightened all in one, promising to go to see us both, Caitlin and me (the baby daughter).

Of course, I knew what was going to happen next. He did go to St Mary Abbot's Hospital and as she saw him outlined in the doorway of the ward, Mum snatched me up and hid us in the bathroom. "Would you believe it," I told my present day friends, "He turned up in his striped pyjamas, dressing gown and slippers. He'd run out of clean clothes with my mother away." My friends were still watching Dylan as he gathered himself together and took the arm Nicolette offered...he'd get a bottle of whisky as a peace offering, he promised. I thought it indelicate to let them know of my presence and anyway it was a long time ago and I` watched them walk somewhat unsteadily towards Manresa Road, Chelsea where my aunt would help him to the studio flat under the bombs of 1943 that was our home then.

Going back to Laugharne

It took Laugharne a long time to realise what had happened to it before it started stocking its paper shop with Dylan Thomas books, Dylan Thomas Caedmon records, prints of Laugharne castle (Dylan Thomas lived in Castle House at one time).

"Duw,duw, if it isn't Miss Thomas?" said an old man, flanked by a younger sports shirted man who said in an American accent, "Is that Dylan Thomas's daughter, did you say? *Very* glad to meet you, Miss Thomas, this is a great honour. I can't say I knew him, exactly..." The "him" is said in reverential tones. "Though we did share an elevator once."

Even the sleepy old pub where my father and mother once drank and socialised, called Brown's Hotel, has a memento. The framed photograph placed above the very table that the Thomases drank at, seems magnificently dated. The clothes they are wearing have changed today, but the alcoved windows behind them are the same.

Photographs are not sold at the pub. They are sold at the paper shop with postcards of the Boat House, the family home. Other one-time abodes of my father's (and there were many due to the nomadic lifestyle of the Bohemian in those days) are sold amongst the cigarettes, newsprint and groceries. However, it took an Australian to take full advantage of the tourists tripping into the paradise that Laugharne has become for fans of the poet. The foreigner came, saw and won with an emporium of literary commerce, the change practically humming along the wires as in *Under Milk Wood's* emporium. The literary goodies and their by-products include Welsh weave though anyone less Nationalistic than my father (much to the chagrin and ensuing insults of the Nationalists) it would be hard to find from such pure Welsh stock: a mother from the farms around Llanstephan, an academic father from the railroads near Swansea with a liberal sprinkling of Welsh hwyl in his articulate and literary ancestry. I think the Nationalists could never forgive my father for excelling in English and not Welsh.

"Come and have a cup of tea," invites the old gentleman. "Myfanwy is waiting..," and hardly without a pause, as we make our way across the large square near the sea end of town, "Proper gentleman your father, mind," he said, as if casting aside much comment to the contrary, "Always saluted me, as he comes along the road..." For him, as most in Laugharne, this could have happened just yesterday for time is a malleable abstraction, a mere follower, never a leader. "And Jean, on account of her serving at the Brown's, she knew him quite well," he continued. "Proper lady your mother was too. Though no holding her back once she started. I never saw her mind doing anything she shouldn't, myself. All talk, I don't wonder." The American, with eager beaver intentness, mouth falling open with the wonderment of it all, took mental notes in excited scrawl. "Shocking use of language, too, I heard," said the old man. "Yes, yes," I said coldly. "Oh, but they were revered, here." Then added, undecided how to appease me, "Just one of us." The old man would have said anything to avoid what the Welsh call "unpleasantness."

I still looked doubtful, remembering that the Laugharne town council, all "old friends", voted again and again at the town meetings not to have the cliff walk named after my father. This is the path that runs directly above the Boat House. Pressure from the ever-growing number of visitors to Laugharne, those who make a special pilgrimage to visit the places where the great poet lived, wrote, and drew his inspiration, finally overruled the local animosity. The path was called "Dylan's Walk" many years after his death.

"Do you remember..." asks Myfanwy. "And when we..." I accept a cup of tea from Sunday crockery with still a trace of dust on the saucer's edge. "Thank you so much," I say mealy mouthed with Welsh cake filling every corner. I am prevaricating in order not to answer immediately. "Do you remember playing with...?" The truth is that some I remember with uncanny clearness, others hardly at all. In their case, time has brought great clouds over my memory like Dai Bread's Wife No. 2 experienced in *Under Milk Wood* when she peered into her crystal ball, into the future. I find looking back much more difficult. "Shocking isn't it," I hear from afar, and am called back to the damp closeted present of the true Welsh parlour and to Laugharne and to the friends that I would always remember. "There's that Dai, now," goes on Myfanwy, untroubled by my silence, "who sets himself up nice and tidy for the rest of the year." She went on to explain, "When he sees the coachloads of Americans coming, and they only come in the Summer months and not in the Winter, he's there quick as a shot with his bunch of lies. Says he know Dylan well, and calls him Dylan mind you, and says this is what Dylan said to him...always the pack of lies he tells them...not daft...so as not to be caught out, see. And that is what Dylan said to his wife, oh *she* knew him as well, according to him of course, and how his children used to play with the Thomas children. "*Well...* do *you* remember them playing with us? He says they used to play with us at the Boat House, down the Grist and up at Orchard Park. And the cheek of it is that he's from Llandeilo. Wasn't even here when your father was alive."

To escape the unused parlour and the dusty particles in the mothballed air, I suggest: "Let's go and see these Americans then," in my version of a Welsh accent. I lost my accent years ago, about thirty years ago, to be exact, when I left Laugharne for a boarding school in Hertfordshire.

We walk to the wide square at the bottom end of town, sea level, and directly under the imposing castle walls known locally as the Grist. A great expanse of mudflats, dotted with down-at-heel rowing boats borders the square. The green bulbous water plants provide a raggedy green carpet under the feet of the castle which you feel might walk away across the grey-green estuary were it not anchored there by long ivy tendrils. It is just as I remember it, three decades ago, except for the coaches parked there in the shade of the castle wall. I imagine a guide getting out of one of the coaches there, finger pointed, arms outstretched, declaiming: "Less than five hundred souls inhabit the three quaint streets and the few narrow by-lanes and scattered farmsteads that constitute this small decaying watering place" and on and on in my father's words from his famous play for voices, *Under Milk Wood*, which was based on Laugharne, "which may, indeed, be called a 'backwater of life' without disrespect to its natives who possess, to this day, a salty individuality of their own..."In reality, the coaches I can see in front of me are empty, their occupants

23

presumably scattered all over Laugharne at the Under Milk Wood Cafe, along Dylan's Walk or at Dylan's Bar. That is except for two earnest ladies now descending from one of the coaches, now looking around them to survey the Grist, the Castle and the Boat House (a speck in the distance) and now perusing a book of poems and prose by my father in hopes that therein they might find the secrets of Laugharne.

"Hello, Miss Thomas," I hear through thoughts, "It is Miss Thomas, then? You haven't changed a bit." Another person comes up to me, vaguely remembered but with no name. I escape to my father's grave at the local churchyard to be accosted again. "I'd recognise you anywhere: image of your father. Yes, yes," to an overseas visitor, "This is the great man's daughter."

"Do you remember the times we used to play on the rocks, jumping over the gaps like flippin' monkeys. Oh, I couldn't do that now. But my children go over to the Boat House when it's fine to play like, and look at all the visitors. And running along the wall around the Boat House as we did, remember. I come over all cold when I think of it. Oh, I'd never allow my children to do it." Myfanwy recalls times past as we sip warm lager in the Brown's.

"See that photo," someone says to me, "You look just like them. You've taken after your father *and* your mother, as I remember them." I turn and recognise one of the locals talking. "We'd sit at the table, the one in the photo, and play cards and dominoes," he said. "Your mother and father were youngsters then. I can remember it like it were yesterday. Mind you, he never spoke poetry to us. I remember there were Ebbie and Ivy, the owners of Brown's then, both dead now, and your grandpa from across the road, may he rest in peace. He lived in The Pelican then, you remember that." I did remember. The Pelican is still there: a tall building, part of a terrace, a garage one side of it. "Or they'd come across from the garage, mun, to be with Mr and Mrs Thomas. When the pub were closing, they'd all move into the kitchen at the back as 'private guests' of Ebbie and Ivy and they'd be up till three or four many a night. Duw, but Mr Thomas could tell a story and your mother not far behind, and we'd be there, the regulars like, exchanging 'hanecdotes' half the night."

Myfanwy took my arm to steer me away, reluctant to let me go. It was she who had first suggested meeting in the pub. "There's nowhere else to go in Wales, of an evening."

"Remember", she said, "How you gave Maggie the new plastic purse you'd got for your birthday if only she'd come over to play with you after school. Oh, you were a terror for giving things."

The old man I first met came up to me, the American still with him. "Well, if it isn't Miss Thomas again," said the American. "This is a pleasant surprise. Can I get you a drink? Is this your friend, will she have one? And my kind guide?" he turned towards his companion. Everyone assented. The old man lent my way, with unwelcome intimacy: "I remember holding you on my knee the day you fell off your bike and we had to call Dr Jenkins over. What a crybaby you were. Proper screamer. Never heard such a lot of blubbering in my life..." (That's *it*, I thought, I'll *never* visit Laugharne again.) "And the way you carried on when the doctor came!" (I remember him, I thought, he was the doctor whom my mother swore only prescribed Calamine lotion whatever the complaint.) "Quite surprised I was," he continued to the rapidly increasing audience that was gathering around, "when he stitched her up she didn't say a word, only looked at him with her eyes sort of popping out." (I would most definitely not be coming here again. All were looking at me as if I were a rarefied animal from the zoo providing a spectacle for them in spite of my small, very unspectacular person.) "Have another drink, Miss Thomas," offered the American. "No thank you," I said with prudish lips, resolving never to come back to Laugharne if I had to listen to such outpourings again. "Do you come here often?" he asked. "Ever thought of living here? I come down every Summer. My main interest is reading and listening to your father's works."

Myfanwy's dad, uncle or grandfather hooked me again by the simple expedient of sitting himself between me and the American. "Oh, you live in Surrey," the American went on valiantly. "Yes, she lives near London," said the old man, with a hint of pride that someone form Laugharne had got that far. Myfanwy now nudged me in the other direction, "Meet Derek," she said. "Grown up a bit, hasn't he. You remember," she nudged with meaning. "Up in the wood shed you and Derek." My mind reeled, made a jump into a remote past but when details appeared, withdrew hastily. (See what I mean, I said to myself, see what I mean. I should never have come back here.) Derek smiled. One of his charms could hardly be his teeth which were now blackened and chipped.

The funny thing is, I find myself going back again and again.

Photo: Courtesy of Colin Shewring

50 years later and more

The Boat House shop still stocks Dylan Thomas books, Dylan Thomas tapes (taken from the original Caedmon 78's), prints and paintings of the house and estuary. The visitors to the museum buy frantically taking home a slice of water and cliff.

The other stockist, situated on the main street that takes you in and out of Laugharne, takes orders through the internet, does business by e-mail, their customers consulting the world-wide web for Dylan Thomas titles. Dylan Thomas books, hardback and paperback, are honoured by the owner in the shopfront coddled by the warm waves of paraffin heaters.

"Is that Miss Thomas, are you married, do you have another surname, so wonderful to meet you, never thought I'd be so lucky, Dylan's daughter did you say, what an honour, delighted I'm sure," says a customer quickly purchasing a book for me to sign.

I move surreptitiously, words wafting around me , to cross the road for the Brown's Hotel. On the steps, is a woman from Lancashire, word has got around, could I stop for a photo. Children appear magically, conjured from behind the columns of Dylan's favourite watering hole, to be included in this literary tableau. I smile as the bored husband appears from the bar. Even his face alights with this photo opportunity. After all, I see in their faces, this might be the last time she appears, she must be knocking on, how old was her father when he died - how old was she in '53?

On entering the Brown's finally, expecting to see the landlord, old and gnarled like the furniture, I make a discovery. The pub is bare. No table where the Thomases drank at, no chairs, no photos on the wall to prove it, just nothing. I'd forgotten, the Brown's Hotel is up for auction.

Well, onto the graveyard then, I mutter, past the hairdresser run by a childhood friend.

At the graveyard, the hill slopes like an amphitheatre so I can see the wooden cross with my mother's name before toiling up the slope to see my father's name on the other side. When my few ashes join their bones, they'll have to inscribe my name in miniletters like an annotation or afterthought. (Oh good, there are fresh flowers organised by me and placed there by the Boat House ladies during the tourist season. I sweep up the plastic tulips strewn across the grave, place them in a carrier bag I brought for that very reason to dump in the refuse bin on my way down). I lower my head for a rapid prayer, the action stronger than my words, just time to wonder whether next time I'll be carried there in an urn. Meantime, cheer up, I say to myself, I'm off to meet Dicky the Milk.

"Naughty man your father", he said, as we sip whisky from tumblers, "to suggest that I watered down the milk. 'Half dew it is,' your father said in *Under Milk Wood*. Oh, I was a very young man when I first delivered the milk to your home on a cart with jugs and ladles. The Boat House had its own jug which you kept in the cold larder away from the mice".

After another tot of whisky, I leave his one-time dairy to cross the road again to the other beyond-recognition establishment: It is the New Mariners taken over by the Notting Hill mafia with ruthless style and money that talks. Being a Londoner myself, I appreciate the improvements: one end a café with tables to drink and chat at, tasteful local stone floors and a corner for loud locals who joke and tumble on alien leather armchairs. I quickly forget this is Laugharne until I recognise the barman, son of Shelagh, my chief playmate in childhood.

Warmed by my six o'clock gin and tonic with posh ice and lemon, I wander outside again, up Victoria Street past Seaview, that tall house my parents lived in before I was thought of and past the Cliff Walk landmarks.

I tiptoe past the writing shed because I see my mother coming my way - no peeping through the keyhole or playing with my bicycle bell. This time she pats my head absent mindedly as she has more pressing things to do nowadays. "See you in a while," she shouts at the shed, as my father works inside, writing at his desk, viewing the estuary birds before him. He sticks his head out of the door, "Oh, Cat!" and she stops to see what he wants. It's only more Woodbines from the general store. I hasten my pace - it'll be me sent on the errand if I don't make myself scarce.

Carefully, I climb down to our front door at sea level. In a moment I'll push the front door open and pass the visitors at the door paying for their entrance tickets into our one-time home. But would you believe it, my brother Llewelyn waits for me, indignant that his bedroom is now a shop with local women selling tickets, information and anything to do with Dylan, his father. Someone has taken his collection of seahorses off the walls, his precious collection of birds' eggs are nowhere to be seen on the shelves of biographies, collected poems and recordings. "Calm down, " I say through the years that separate us, "You don't need this room where you are now."

Will you sign the visitors' book again?" ask the girls on the till, "It's years since you first did it... when the Council took over, remember." I am shown my younger brother's signature and am glad Colm might be asked to sign again on his next visit though he won't be able to better his first message: "Nice place to live here," he wrote and what he said was true for all of us.

◇◇◇

Photos: Courtesy of Reg Evans

Dylan's parents, D.J. Thomas and Mrs Florence Thomas

Later than Laugharne

Herons, mussel pools, gulls and pipers,
encircle our "house on stilts high among
beaks and palavers of birds". Cormorants
scud and gulls glide in my memory.
The stones, washed by the tide, which I
would turn looking for blue and white,
or floral pieces of china for our crockery
houses... And the fish my mother would
catch and throw back into the swirling

Photo: Thompson Press

*Aeronwy reading to her son Huw from one of the books she
received from her father at Christmas.*

waters of the estuary all around us ...
I remember them well.
... And high tide covering our back garden
through a hole in the stone wall which
embraced our home. The tide carrying our
makeshift boats on its back, pieces of lumber,
an old zinc bath, and I can still recall
the envy I felt when they bought my brother
a boat called The Cuckoo...
The names come tumbling back –
... And I remember the hole in the wall was
called grandly by all, The Harbour.
... And who could forget sliding down the
mud banks at low tide into the rivulets
left by the receding water, or running along
the cliffwalk and stirring up a din outside
the shed that was my father's writing den.
The memories race back –
... And the thrill of peeping through
the keyhole (I was always the most naughty)
to see my father writing his poems about
gulls, hills and cormorants on estuaries
which he saw through his wide-vista window,
as he sat, bent, writing in crabbed letters,
pressing against the hard surface of the
kitchen table that was his desk...
We were poor those days –
Though I can't remember being poor
in Laugharne, in those balmy,
never-to-be-forgotten days,
green and golden...

Herons, gulls and pipers still encircle
our house on stilts,
and the cormorants still scud and glide
in my memory...

Aeronwy Thomas

The Boat House, overlooking the estuary.

Photos: Courtesy of Colin Shewring